BOOKS BY LAURIE SHECK

THE WILLOW GROVE

THE
WILLOW GROVE

POEMS BY

LAURIE SHECK

ALFRED A KNOPF

NEW YORK

1996

THIS IS A BORZOI BOOK
PUBLISHED BY ALFRED A. KNOPF, INC.

Grateful acknowledgment is made to the following magazines in which these poems first appeared:

AGNI REVIEW: From "The Book of Persephone" (I)
COLUMBIA: "Sea," "Marionettes," "The Wood Lily, Etc.," "The Stockroom," "White Light," "Black Night"
MANY MOUNTAINS MOVING: From "The Book of Persephone" (IV)
THE MICHIGAN QUARTERLY REVIEW: "Mannequins"
THE NEW YORKER: "White Noise," "The Return," "The Inn"
THE PARIS REVIEW: "Filming Jocasta"
PLOUGHSHARES: "Living Color," "Rain"
THE PLUM REVIEW: From "The Book of Persephone" (VII) and (IX)
RIVER STYX: "Headlights"
SALAMANDER: "Mummy"
THE SENECA REVIEW: From "The Book of Persephone" (VI), "The Unfinished"
SOUTHERN HUMANITIES REVIEW: From "The Book of Persephone" (III)

"Living Color" was included in Best American Poetry 1991, edited by Mark Strand and David Lehman (New York: Collier Books, 1992).

"Mannequins" was included in The Pushcart Prize: Best of the Small Presses, 1992, edited by Bill Henderson (New York: Pushcart Press, 1993).

I would like to thank the Guggenheim Foundation whose generous support afforded me valuable time and encouragement to work on this book, and the New Jersey State Council on the Arts for poetry fellowships in 1990 and 1993.

"February Morning" is for Jim Peck. "In Spring" is for Maia Peck, and "The Harbor Boats" is for Dr. David Mayer.

Library of Congress Cataloging-in-Publication Data

Sheck, Laurie.
    The willow grove:poems/by Laurie Sheck.—1st ed.
        p.   cm.
   ISBN 0–679–44714–8
    I. Title.
PS3569.H3917W55   1996   96–4147
811'.54—dc20   CIP

To Harry Ford

. . . and when she has brought you across the River of Ocean, you will come to a wild coast and Persephone's Grove, where the tall poplars grow, and the willows that so quickly shed their seeds.

HOMER, *The Odyssey*

When Persephone took her place on Hades' throne and her scented face peeped out from behind the spiky beard of her partner, when Persephone bit into the pomegranate that grew in the shadow gardens, death underwent a transformation every bit as radical as that which life had undergone when it had been deprived of the girl. The two kingdoms were thrown off balance, each opening up to the other. Hades imposed an absence on earth, imposed a situation where every presence was now enveloped in a far greater cloak of absence. Persephone imposed blood on the dead: not, as in the past, the dark blood of sacrifice, not the blood the dead used to drink so thirstily, but the invisible blood that went on pulsing in her white arms, the blood of someone who is still entirely alive, even in the palace of death.

ROBERTO CALASSO, *The Marriage of Cadmus and Harmony*

The upward movement in us is in vain (and less than vain) if it does not come from a downward movement.

SIMONE WEIL, *Gravity and Grace*

Contents

Contents

THE WILLOW GROVE

White Noise

The faces are lifted up into the jumpy light,
the blue electric glow
buzzing them forward into closeup
until the foreground is their eyes, and the fear that is their eyes,
        and tangled hair,
and mouths that grief has torn, clawed open.

(I am lying on a couch in a city that is shadows and glass
and shadows of skyscrapered glass,
that is steel and more steel and billboards
where tall white legs are splayed against white sand, blue surf,
and the red mouths, presiding high above the moving crowds,
are lipsticked, smiling, smooth, and waiting for a cigarette.)

The TV flickers, grays, the faces are gone now
into the undertow
of hunger for the next thing and the next.

(I am lying in a city that is a text unwriting itself,
that is a coffin of glass and a statue of glass,
and the words *why hast thou*, and the words *how many* and *what number*,
and *thy Father which is in secret*, and *thy Father
which seeth in secret*.)

And after the news is over the jokes start up,
the studio audience clapping on cue, pre-recorded, the theme music
        rising,
the wait right there we'll be back in a minute,
the screen swallowing, swallowing, until there's an anthem,
a test pattern, darkness, and only a pinprick of light breaking through.

And somewhere outside of all that are overhead lights and the shutting
        of lights,
there are rows of windows stacked like crates
in the darkness, good night and good night,
and the loneliness that is what's left of the dream of beauty
in which the eyes come back to haunt the empty screen,
the eyes and the hands beneath them
and the mouth saying,

"When I suffer, I cannot forget that I am, nor fail to know
that I am nothing."

The Return

And then he entered the city: in the old stories,
when the hero returns, it is clear where the city begins—
he walks through the arched gateway
cut through the surrounding walls, and he is home.
But now it is more a matter of thickness and thinness:
doorways crowd toward each other like perilous hunched shoulders,
windows harden and multiply, vertical and bright.

Here the sky is reddish brown at nightfall
beneath what we still think of as the stars.
Newspapers blow in gutters,
the drained faces of victims and statesmen
press against the pavement, smudged. Or their hands
are lost in the rainbowed oil of passing cars;
the black ink bleeds.

And the people are passing, the crowds of them, so busy,
as if we were still alive—are we alive?
Maybe a questionnaire will lead us to some answer.
It wants to know: How many push-button phones do you have?
Do you use call-forward? Have you purchased a car phone
within the last six months?

The skyscrapers rise pale green and silver,
as if nothing could ever make them burn.
The phones lie in their cradles, sleeping.
I meant to call when I arrived;
is your name still buried in the phone book under "A,"
pressed between the other, similar last names,
laid down there in print deep black as the wires
that carry one human voice to another?

Someone has painted black shadows, human, groping,
eyeless on this alley's dirty walls.
I touch each faceless face, like frost.

The Stockroom

I watch the boy shoot up.
His head woozes back, eyes fluttering lightly
into what land, what dreamy repetition, separateness, deferment,
grainy black and white of this sleep that is not sleep?
He closes his eyes but I still watch. I am a child, I do not know
     who he is,

or how he's wandered back
into the stockroom of this store. I am supposed to be up front
where it is light, helping to sell buttons, pencils, keys.
I am supposed to walk around in the safe glare,
the sharp-edged present tense.
But here in this dim room behind the aisles

the boy crawls slowly toward a wall
that used to be part of the bakery next door—brick ovens three
     feet deep
with rounded tops like quaint old-fashioned doorways,
crumbling now, and damp, his head swaying like a battered stalk.
He leans back into the oven-dark and shivers,
scratches his cheek with one hand and then the other;

he smooths his itchy skin, scaly, purplish-red.
What tense is it he drifts in? What tense in which memories rise up
disguised so they won't stun, mixing with this musty air,
these towers of cardboard boxes held in the eerie sway
of so much want? What tense in which we sit,
the boy and I, and do not speak, the dark like a god

and our small bodies like errors
the god wants to take back again, out of his created world?
And what tense in which the musty dampness holds the ovens
like moldy unrocked cradles, eye-holes, graves,
and street-cries skip and flare above our listening, but they are
     muffled
from back here, as if they could not touch us, yet still here?

The drawers of the cash registers clack open again and again
like solved equations, while the boy breathes so softly,
his hands clutched into fists now
as if trying to protect something hidden, keep it safe.
There is the dark of his closed hands, there is the oven-dark,

and then the larger stockroom dark. I think there is no tense for this—
how he rubs his palms into his eyes

then slides his bony shoulders and thin face toward the light
of the narrow doorway, the long aisles
just out of sight, and then turns slowly back.
Land of transactions, of tactics, sirens, cries—

it is what waits outside this dark and doesn't want to know this dark.
Aisles of clocks, of kitchenware, venetian blinds.
He looks up from the dimness and damp brick, his eyes drifting—where?—
before me, into what abrogation, what refusal
of earthly terror, earthly place?

From The Book of Persephone (I)

This darkness. And what rises up out of this darkness.

I open the book of lost entries—
how fraudulence moves like a wind through the world,
how there's no page that is not shredded,
and there is nothing pure but a forgotten thing.

I remember nothing. I remember the stars and moon,
the entries I burned and didn't burn, the entries
like crumbled terraces of stars.
Each page of gutted houses, curtains of violence and sighs.
A child's cry pressed in a pillow. The crossed-out words
that haunted the white page, and the syntax clamping down
too hard, like a locked box.
The water murmuring *was was was.*

I remember nothing. It is winter. There is a forest of bare trees,
a town consisting of forged documents
through which a child must walk.
There is a city of cries, the child's sealed mouth, its tired legs.
Out of the dark more dark, razored or soft.

It is winter. The withered gardens whisper their dry stalks.
The child kneels at a locked box. There are walls
that shudder like flea-bitten cloth, there are walls disappearing,
and above them the leaden movie-glow of dusk,
then the hours of larceny, of theft.

I remember nothing. I remember the scattered pages,
the mechanisms of sums, the cities accomplished
and spoiled, crumbling and re-made.
The candor of ruin and the gates. In daylight the businesses
go on, the bright calculations, the frantic advertisements
that masquerade as calm. So little evidence is left
of what has vanished. As if when the swan lifts off the liquid stare
it is the wind of our words it leaves behind.

I remember nothing. I remember soft faces streaked with fear,
the red and gold disclosures stuttering briefly
before they finally closed. And then a darkness falling
downward, all strobe-lit and reeling, then this flat darkness

like the pressure of a hand.

From The Book of Persephone (II)

What song do the hills sing as they whiten?
And the goat that stumbles, falling from the jutting rock?
And what of the river still pulsing its wishes through my skin?
I remember the bevelled hills where I once walked,
rock the color of stars, yellow swathes of wild orchids
by the roadside, but don't know how to move toward them.

My hands are hobbled birds, my lips chapped and swollen.
When my hair falls over my face
I imagine I am not in this world or another,
that a fragrant wind encloses me, sweet lull
in the lingering dampness, though if it's gold
or coal-black I cannot say.

My cloth doll's neck loosens and grows slack.
Clumps of cotton bunch and tear inside her,
her wild hair like a desperate forgetting,
her ravelled clothes shot through with woodsmoke
and damp earth, salt and feathers rotting
in the sun. She dances her still dance
whose story is a forest, a bare field,
contingencies swarming like the woodsmoke
that once touched her,
her face quiet as the stone she lies on.

What is not captive? My fingers
send helpless shadows down the page, thin bars
of useless dark.

There is a dance I do not understand
that the wind does on the wildest hills, and which my presence
diminishes, and my eyes diminish,
as if I am not meant to understand, as if I am a kind of defilement.
I see the branches are meant to take such wildness
but my doll's neck grows weaker, flopping back and forth,
and I think she must disappear soon
as when I saw one day, in summer, a fog move in on three brown horses
and in seconds consume their heavy bodies.

My hands make the shapes of hills. My lips taste the acrid dampness.
Is it morning now? Is it night? Here the darkness
doesn't lengthen or grow less. I listen to the whitening
of the hills. I listen to the way they have grown cold
and cannot wander.

Living Color

At first there's greenish flesh until the knob's
turned farther to the right, and then the flesh turns paler, pink;
the gray walls behind the silent faces
shimmer, and next the sound's turned up,
the lips are moving, the hands, the voices, rising, moving—
is this what fright is, these
pale interchangeable faces,
is this the body of the world
that can be seen but never touched,

the faces floating there, the hands,
and all the broken things?
The set casts its flickering light onto the walls
as the ghost-bodies dressed in their momentary garments
bend to kiss
the gleaming armor of the world.
They have given themselves over
to quickness,
to soundbites, to thirty- or sixty-

second spots.
How slow we are against them
who dream of change but rarely, finally, change.
Now the man is walking toward the woman.
He sits down beside her on the bed,
the walls pale gold,
the bedspread flowered, gold. On her dresser
are many small bottles, delicate long-stemmed
vials, perfume and makeup,

and on the wall above it
a mirror that holds them from behind
showing us what the man and woman cannot see
of who they are: the man's broad back
in his striped suit, the woman barely covered by a negligé,
her brown hair tumbling down.
As if they had no names. As if they had no
faces, no address.
But she lifts her face to him

and her skin is smooth as the gold lamplight
falling in a calm closed circle on the carpet
    so that we are meant to think:
        it is important to know what happens
next. But how grotesque
        they appear when I turn off the sound,
trapped in a world where speech is ceaselessly
        required, in which mouths move and move
        but nothing can come out

    and still they keep on moving
the way neon pulses on and off, on and off
    against a wall. No stillness there. No rest.
        And no one can be left alone for long;
if the woman stands at her window
                it is clear soon enough someone will come knocking
on her door. There is no room
    for silence. I turn off the set.
    I watch the dark blank screen,

    how it holds only the merest shading of a face,
barely there but still it's there,
    no sound at all, no humming sound, no hushed
        electric purr, just blank
like the door a child wakes to in the night,
    the voices shimmering and slurring
on the other side, in darkness,
    but there is no screen to hold them, making them its ghosts,
    there is no way to shut them off.

Poppies

Red poppies, you do not open onto treachery or possession.
I walk among you, where only last spring the grass stiffened white
as a fretful wedding, frost glittering like foil.
Everywhere my hands touched brittleness—bare branches,
gimcracked ice; the air was ether on my skin.

You quiver lightly, and I see that you are not contrary;
you don't hide from the sun your black impenetrable hearts.
And at nightfall you close softly as eyes that are not afraid of sleep,
a child's eyes closing on a murmur, on a lie that doesn't matter.

Now at the field's edge a dog snarls at a rabbit.
A hawk circles, circles, over the bare rock
that stands like a bored sentinel focused on some distant morning.
Soon it will lift the startled field mouse in its claws.

Your red petals do not hiss or whimper.
You are so quiet, opening and closing on an emptiness benign
and frightless. Pressed between finger and thumb
your petals ball into a wet red mass.
But when you're left alone, your crimson silks flame cleanly

in the sun. Even your own fragility doesn't harm you,
doesn't stop the flagrant glow that burns like the moment
beneath a child's lids when the story flares its neon outlines
before sleep, before the windows fully blacken.

Evening Walk

The sky's the color of an x-ray pinned to the viewing light,
the birds crossing and re-crossing it,
their coal-colored wings like the darkened inlets
at the base of the skull where the body hoards
its most secret repositories of iron.

This is the hour when the birds' songs seem most loud,
as if soon they must grow wary, approximate,
a black cloth thrown over them, a heavy floating cloth,
whole armies of hiddenness advancing.

What would the sky be like without them—
without the wavy passage of the wrens
or the redwinged blackbirds lifting from the field's long grass?
I think I would fear its emptiness, its deep untamed forgetfulness,
the faintest hush of a tamped candle.

I walk toward the feeder
where hummingbirds drink the red-tinted sugar water
I boiled for them in my iron pot, stirring it with a wooden spoon.
Their beaks poke into openings ringed with plastic daisies.
They are buzzing backward and forward
like little wind-up toys at a roadside stand.
Where do they sleep? Into what do they enfold themselves?
They whirr and flutter like shot nerves.

All day the clouds over the hill hid the sun,
a deposed queen locked away from her green subjects,
her immaculate possessions. I think the wrens did not miss her;
they have their tasks and the earth is not strange to them
as they fly between branches numerous, supple, and flowering with
        sweetness,
not having sensed it yet — the broken world.

From The Book of Persephone (III)

White grove, white trace of dawn,
your arguments are noiseless, locked.
No tribunal waits for you, it will not
touch you with its verdict,
though I would give you my torn deposition,
you whose stake in this is nothing.

I have heard my voice played back from the tape recorder
scorched with distance, as if I did not own it,
and the voices of others cut into segments,
soundbites like paperclips holding the blown pages.
I have known myself as the dizziness
marring the still sky, causing it to tilt and quiver,
dividing it into wide panels of gray light
that fall and break apart.
Blame is a secret terror.

The radio says: we will keep you abreast
of all fast-breaking developments, we will give you
in-depth coverage. But I think now each story
lies sequestered, convulsed
and palsied under laws of speaking.

All this I carry on my skin: forensic light,
the faintest lines of forfeiture and purchase,
plunder of cover-ups and lies. All this
I carry in each cell: the steady salary of doubt,
the waiting for a gavel to fall
that doesn't fall.

White sycamores, white ash,
here in your fashionless adequacy, you bend down and bend down.
Is there an antidote to stain, to treason?
On my forehead I feel a fever-kiss always,
its famished need of me, its famished wish.
The frost gives up its wayward steps inside you.

Mannequins

Rifle-thin, they stand in their angelic armor.
What love has brought them here, what story,
only to drop them down on this terrain of glass and chrome
smooth as an assassin's mask; cold trophies,
still aftermaths of innocence,
no longer touched by hurry or surprise?

Contagion is another world now, fear
another world. The softness that once held them has long vanished,
the bribes of kindness, dim corridors of night,
swift nets, swift versions, lies.
They thrive like the hard bark of leafless trees.

In their eyes all things are suspect.
The city's deformity, its standard unstoppable vanity,
spreads its glow, like ice, around them.
But they stand cloaked in a further, stranger coldness.
Fierce, telescopic, they wait, the one true dream
beneath the dream.

Out of this blank sleep, no other sleep.
Sinister hinges, the minutes tick.
Their long hair spills down like laughter
constrained behind the bright unyielding glass;
smiles flatten like closed hatches.

All day, all night, as if the city had already turned to ruin,
having brought with it the bombed deserted streets,
crumbled doorways, blasted cars,
they stand stock-still, watching, and feel nothing.
This is the rubble of astonishment, it is astonishment's cold
tomb and the eyes it left there, open, as they froze.

Voltage

So it goes on, this waking to static
and a sense that all the photographs are doctored.
Glass, more glass. Such black distances the bells have travelled.
The minutes pushing forward, and the beautiful abductions,

the horrible abductions.
Planes pass and pass, silver and remote above the skyline,
heading toward destinations that stand fast,
that do not disappear.
This is, they seem to say, *this is*,

and I hear the low groaning of their passage.
So it goes on, this tape or that tape clicking into place,
traffic lights changing on schedule,
a child standing with crumbled petals in her hand.
Someone sings from the bottom of the hill,

their words too far off to understand.
A child unwraps a lantern from blue paper.
I can dial the weather or the time,
I can ask for distant numbers I won't call.
Damage is so quiet. The sparrow drags its crooked wing
and doesn't cry; stale bread crumbs on my windowsill untouched.
It is the other ones that sing now, suggesting a vertical

world, making me look up to find them.
Black wires criss-cross the sky. I walk from room to room
and though the walls do not shift they are no answer.
The wind carries cinders, lifting and swirling
their soft dispersing taint.

The hurt sparrow is the color of the sidewalk,
the color of the dirty sky. It drags itself in circles.
Above it the black wires barely waver
as they channel their invisible voltage through the air.

The Unfinished

We were characters in a story
the writer couldn't bring himself to finish.
When he left us it was late, a child
was crying, newsprint smudged on our fingertips
as if to make of us a mechanism
by which the world would repeat itself, its story:
this happened—did you hear?—then that.
So many disparate versions. The terror
risen into words, shrouded there, hanging, so cold.
And the tenderness—how the words barely touched it,
as if to speak it were a further hurt.
It was night when he left us,
and the child who could not yet remember her dreams
woke saying, *where are the toys of the moon,
are we the moon's toys*? Outside, lines
of stiff trees stood like hieroglyphs,
the configuration of the one for dagger
so close to the one that stands for shrub,
so hard to understand the difference;
or the one for fear that also could mean
reverence, the one for medicine so similar
to entreaty and to prayer.
And in the distance the red tremor
of the radio tower, and the planes that passed above us
as we held to the earth and didn't understand the earth.

The Inn

The air darkens in gradations like a Xeroxed page
the machine is making darker with each copy,
slowly, slowly, until the inner workings grind
finally to a halt, completely broken.

A. lounges in a chair. Here in this strange town
of small thatched cottages and inns, flower gardens,
remnants of medieval walls, she is leafing through a book,
stopping here and there to hold the top corner of a page
the way, as a child, she lifted a butterfly's wing
from the wet grass.

When we were children combing out our hair
before the bathroom mirror
I noticed one morning the light glaring oddly off her head
and saw that a clump of her hair had fallen out.
Why do I remember this now? The doctor found some salve
to help her, though the look of horror
in her eyes when I told her
marked for me the moment I no longer
thought of us as children.

If this is the world, we must find some way
to belong to it.

A. reads to me out loud:
*We live on a forgotten star. Here there are harmful truths
and fruitful errors. How much lies seemingly dead
in magic sleep?*

But I am imagining this, for in reality A. and I
no longer speak. In the airport terminal, a small child
presses his hands against the glass,
then points to the sleek-finned bodies of the jets.
Fish, he says, *fish*. Licked fingers turn the slow pages
of the glossy magazines. I have grown used to the lowering
of my eyes in places such as this
where strangers and volatility intersect so closely.

The book drops from A.'s hand. She is dozing.
Outside the window of the inn
a field lies fallow for planting, and beyond that a hill
where earlier some cows were grazing. *Picturesque*, says the brochure,
though this is someone's life, his rising in the middle of the night.
A.'s face, the architecture of grief or an unresolved forgetting,
floats in a small stillness. There will be no photos to take back.

From The Book of Persephone (IV)

The river is quiet now, and dark, as if inside it
another world were sleeping,
a world a child might dream
in which the stars are not constrained within their farness
but bend to touch the child's skin, its face
moth-gray in the hours before morning.

One night when I was small I peeked into a lamplit room
quiet as this river
to see, through milky glass, the grownups talking.
I thought of the laws they had made,
(they had told me there were laws)
and how those laws hadn't rescued the shivering ones
from their cardboard homes in winter,
or the ones who wandered babbling through the park
conducting an invisible orchestra with a stick,
or the ones who went rummaging through trash cans,
looking, it seemed, not just for food,
but something treasured and lost track of long ago.
The grownups' faces shone in the untroubled light.
How strong they looked,
as if their power

were a form of armor.
But the longer I watched them
the more they became strange creatures to me,
owners of a language I couldn't understand.
What secret sorrows
wandered like gold threads beneath their skin?
What jealousies and falseness?
On the table were long-stemmed glasses,
plates of cheeses and green apples, bottles of red wine.
I walked out to the edge of the field

(though I knew I was supposed to be asleep)
to touch the trees that knew no human laws,
no secrets encircling them like wire.
How frail the house looked from that distance,
the portraits on its walls
remote and small as postage stamps
on envelopes that soon would be discarded.
So that I thought the ones inside talked not for company

but for shelter,
not wanting to look down at their hands, in the night, alone,
where each year the blue veins rose more plainly
toward the skin's mottled surface.

I knew a lamb slept in the shed. Walking back to the house
I thought I heard it crying, bleating
as if it were in pain, and I imagined the night carving
a terrible bright eye onto its body,

an eye that couldn't close, and couldn't ever be removed.

From The Book of Persephone (V)

There is no wind in these trees at all,
no shadows stirring in the willow grove and poplars
the way the first glimmerings of loss
begin to form inside a child's body. . . .

Once, long ago, I was taken to a room
filled with hundreds of clay statues,
some as small as my fist (I was a child),
others as tall as I was then.
But each one was composed of the same figures—
a mother and her infant child.
Each woman's arms looked casual, relaxed,
as she held the tiny child in her lap,
and yet there seemed in the stiff fingers
a hidden desperation. The infants' eyes

were very wide. Maybe they are afraid to go to sleep, I thought,
or maybe being so new to the earth
they don't trust the strangeness
to not harm them. Each child's face looked straight ahead.
Many of the mothers' heads were chipped
or broken wholly off;
they had lain so long inside the earth or on its surface.
But even the headless ones still clutched the tiny child
whose head leaned back against the waiting chest.
A book had been left open on a lectern,

the pages showing pictures of how the statues
had once been—painted vivid blues and golds
as if the sky had come alive inside them.
Stars and crescent moons glowed on their robes.
One of the infant children held a little bird
in his cupped palm, though now, in the room, his palm was empty,
and I wondered what song still pierced his body.
Over and over I turned the brittle yellowed pages

that held no hint of defilement,
or the lies that proceed from the need to wield power
over another, or the daily bits of news,
the world tilting farther and more sharply
toward each body, or how the meanings of words
can confuse for a child

the stark untroubled lines of a young tree.
I watched and watched as I held each gilt-edged page—
each page so frail and without context
where over and over the children's eyes
looked out into that chilly room
as if to find some world to cling to.

The Wood Lily, Etc.

A hiddenness sang to me, lured me in. I heard it even in daylight,
even in the strongest sun. It was louder than the pharmacist's
vat of pills I saw him dividing into so many labelled bottles
with their child-safe caps. Sir, here is my prescription,
its dosage, re-fills, times.

Listening, I heard its lexicon: gun barrel, factory, sanctum,
interior of the honeysuckle, moonseed, whorl of conch.
The way the lush world closes.
The wood lily at evening, the catch in the asthmatic's throat.
My hands closing on nothing.

Over the road the cars pass in slanting rain, leaving a breathy hiss
where their tires slick so quickly. Then the air begins to clear,
opening onto TV light, onto light flung down from the willow,
light glinting off a child's toy, off grease on the freezer,
while the trees bend as if to dissolve inside themselves,

as if the wind were closing them, a book, a riven text
someone is murmuring the words of before heading off to work.
But as I'm watching, the wind begins to open them also,
unfolding itself from their branches,
so that it seems they are becoming and dissolving all at once,

opening and closing, themselves and not themselves.
And when they open I think: aperture, puncture wound, spillage,
each one a lexicon of uncovering. And how sunlight slices the page
or wavers there, in its nervous materiality, rocking.
I think: lock-picker, safe-cracker, shadowed inlet of the unclenched rose.

Lexicon of tracings and disclosures, of doorways leading onto alleyways
and courtyards, and of the night-blooming cereus spreading its smooth
petals on the hill, I move toward you like the boy who blinded himself
accidentally one cold winter morning, and now rises after months
from his sickbed to touch the curious redeeming braille.

Marionettes

From behind the painted cardboard village
they drop down and rise up
as if gravity didn't own them,
their bows decomposing the stillness
as rows of lit windows shed quietness
onto the grass. There are footfalls, bells,
skirts twirling under flowering trees.

Exposure doesn't scare them.
They push out beyond the stare
of fear, lifting up past the silly rules
the hands that guide them live by.
They want only to give themselves away,
outlaws from each cautionary trance,
enemies of stillness.

Quick music from a fiddle eyes you.
Come here, it says, come in.
Gardens carry flowers into cupboards of night.
Whose village is this? Whose air uncut by static?
Their wooden skin can't hear the roar of the expressway.
Like a reporter in a foreign land, you watch them.

And when they are put down
and wound round in their white strings,
the red case that holds them closed,
they are a sequestered jury
that has deliberated long, and fought,
and passed its verdict,
but can speak it only to themselves.

In Spring

I carried the baby on my back over the steep flagstone streets,
the gold light falling with such calmness
as it skimmed the flowered walls and low stone arches,

whereas once, it is said, a great invasion occured here
and from a wall a saint's wounded face bled deeply from forehead to chin.
When a man tried to staunch it his right hand shriveled
and went weak, his right foot dried up, and until the day he died
his whole body continued to wither, until he lay completely paralyzed.
And so the story went that this was how the saint displayed its anger
at an attempt to cover up its outraged grief,
the horror it did not choose to hide.
Later there would be more invasions, occupations,

submissions and exiles and returns from exile,
and in between each devastation, the flourishing markets, houses swan-white
or sandstone, systems for warehousing and gathering water,
terraces facing the sea.

From the cliff we could look down at the green water,
eels flashing in a quick unbidden freedom.
Green and orange seaweeds swayed. The baby reached out her hands,
grabbing fistfulls of air. . . .

We'd driven down through a countryside known for its hundreds
of abandoned crumbling towers, dry fields divided by rock fences.
It was said to be the *land of the mistrustful*
where for centuries each family monitored from its tower
the actions of the others, until, over time, the place became deserted.

We'd stayed the night in a tower the government had restored,
a cave-like room with whitewashed walls, and a trap door on the ceiling
where a ladder could take you from one story to another.
Wild dogs lived in the hills, and keening wind.
And on the dry surrounding precipices, prickly pear grew, and razor
　　　grass, and fig trees.

But now, as we walked the steep flowered streets,
it seemed we had entered a small pocket of gold light,
a quiet fragment of held light,
not the whole of what there is, not the whole of it at all,
but a part like the ripped corner of one beautiful illuminated page.

The Visit

From its bed of hay
the small goat lifts its mild eyes
to see us. Just this morning its horns have been sawn off.
It lies in the barn of this farm
we are visiting, where barbed wire is strung in silver arcs
over rows of raspberries to keep the birds
from swooping down to eat them, and where the old red tractor
is a child's toy now, painted with marigolds and daisies.
The goat looks up at you who are so small
and tilts its head as if in recognition.
                              I remember once watching a deer
being born, its legs brittle kindling.
How the afterbirth hung from the mother
as she nudged the wet fawn with her nose
to stand and walk. The father jumped suddenly back
letting out a wild cry, turning violently away
from its child. The fawn tried to rise;
stumbled, wobbled, fell. The mother shoved it
with her head, hard, almost angry.
Are fawns born with their eyes already open?
Why can't I remember its eyes? I remember
the legs, twiggy and blood-covered,
and how it didn't try to nurse, only to stand
again and again as was required, while the wind
clicked on like an answering machine
playing over and over a horrible white noise.
                              You want to pet the goat,
to touch the place its horns have been sawn off.
You want to feel if it is rough or smooth
where it was cut. And why is there no blood?
I watch your fingers reach for it
as the goat offers its head to you
and I step back; you pet it lightly, lightly,
as if to learn by braille this soft
imprisonment that claims us.

Childhood

The diamond-patterned store gates screech open as my father unlocks them,
shoving them back from the plate glass windows and double-bolted doors,
and I am led by a hand into the unlit cavern of the store.
I watch the lights switch on, until, beneath them, shelf upon shelf
of merchandise takes shape and glistens: rows of porcelain bulls
glazed blazing red or black with gold-tipped horns, and saucers, cups,
clocks on the wall whose cat-faces hum
while their tails slice back and forth with a mad metronomic precision,
and the cash register sits like an angry closed-mouthed woman.
Here's how you can tell who'll probably shop-lift,

my father says, and shows me (I am seven) how junkies scratch their
hollow cheeks, and how the whites of their eyes film over, yellow-red.
It is my job to follow them up and down the aisles,
my child-eyes already trained for surveillance.
Nights I dream their sweat seeping like rain through plaster walls,
their twitching, shaking hands desperate for something to hold.
In fluorescent light I walk the aisles with a feather-duster,
        listening to the words
that sing like wind-blown leaves above me: you quiero, mi madre,
        cuanto, por favor, no mas.
But the day the beautiful woman comes in, gliding between

the matrons in brown shifts and the children brought along
        to translate
for their parents, I stop my dusting and just watch.
Her long black hair shimmers brightly like the porcelain bulls;
she is wearing a fur coat and long earrings, her skin the lucent sheen
of a black tulip. She seems untouched by the dirt I swirl up
on myself as I dust, and that my father carries home each night on his
        khaki work clothes.
Quickly she buys some picture hooks, and leaves.
You know that was a man, my father says, as I watch her

cross the busy street and head up Prospect Avenue,
past the boys leaning and clicking their tongues from the corner.
I go back to my dusting. That woman is a man, I think, a man.
I imagine her elegant hands touching a tenement wall, running a finger
down the crack she'll cover with a picture,
or touching the hand of a junkie, the one I followed as he stole

a gold expensive key chain. I should have told but didn't tell,
as I pictured it gleaming in his pocket
like something medicinal or holy,
a buried treasure such as children keep in the dresser drawers
of their bedrooms, as if that hidden gleaming thing
could listen and protect them, encircling them with kindness as they sleep.

Learning to Read

I know there is something that mocks us, and it is cold and distant and
    cannot
be hurt. Even the grownups' hands are small against it.
More and more Night twines its ragged threads into my hair;
I hear the wracked branches, ruined stars.

But here, in the primer, it is different.
The sun is yellow. Its face is round, and smiles.
The leaves are oval, green. And beneath them five letters clump together
forming the word *green* so that it stays like a metal toy train on the
    whiteness.
As if it didn't ever want to leave. It must have travelled far

to get here, and now, its engine stilled,
it lingers beneath a sky steady, blue, and safe.
For now the words are orderly—black barrels, lacquered boxes, shelves,
each page an outstretched palm holding a dollhouse's willfully protected
    treasures.
For now they take me in where the brokenness can't find me.
The house is red. The cat is gray. The girl is running and jumping in
    the grass.

I do not know yet how the words will hiss and tremble on other, fuller
    pages,
how they'll shatter and creak, or how they'll harbor an unspeakable
    wildness
inside them like a bird crazily flinging itself against plate glass.
Or how they'll become an insomniac's wandering tale,
and hands into which I must place again and again
the remote and human blankness of my hands.

These are the deep black shapes of remembrance and forgetting.
Years, and the pages thicken with more words, becoming a forest,
a maze of displacement, a wrecked lullaby, a beautiful and fierce
    derailment.
Becoming a child's face forever staring through a window's shattered
    glass;
a murderer's knife, a slashed canvas, deepest black of disfigurement
and healing. Soft lips on a forehead leaving no trace of their kiss.
Gravestones in snow. A mouth obsessively unnaming what it's known.

From The Book of Persephone (VI)

Grass fronds, leaves in wind. The light smooth
and then shattering. There are fragments, shards,

distortions of shadows, birds.

(I am distant from myself I watch myself shatter.)

Beautiful light, sunlight on branches, on water, I think,
and lilies, crocuses, poppies, wild roses,
birds, grass, grass, water—

but they are gone from me now, those things,
now there is only this distance from the world.

(So this is how the skin flares up into bitterness,
this fear like toxic waste,
this numbness rubbing its oils into my palms.)

First there was sunlight, then darkness, then this farness
sifting down onto my skin: my skin listening, each pore of me
listening. There was a dream in which a fire burned
and then the dream of mourning.

Once upon a . . . once upon a time . . . then nothing.
I am under the Well of the Beautiful Dances,
under the stiff sheets of fallen leaves.

Above me they are dancing—the girls with bridal veils
and the children spilling their baskets
of loosestrife and dried grass. They are twirling bright scarves
and long white capes. The earth they dance on
has grown barren: no barley, wasted fields.

Someday I think I will go back there
but how will I believe in my own skin, what it can touch, what it can know?
This dream of skin, this scorched enchanted dream.
What is belonging? Into what does the dream vanish when we waken?
Where is its hiding place? Where is the ghost of its waking on my skin?

Mummy

Mummy-girl, unearthed now, your wrappings fraying, gray,
your hands stiff with vigilance,
we have not let you go. The waters purl and sway beyond you.
My glassy face in the case above you
watches. Outside the cars go by, their sounds touching you

like poisons. You who meant to stay so far away, to stay so deeply
hidden. But we lifted you out of your hiding place
where the papyrus buried beside you held the words you would have spoken
as you journeyed from this earth: *I am the knot within the olive tree,*
the branch of the tamarisk, beautiful, gone forth and going forth.
No harm will come to me. My face is open, my wishes are all open,
O never setting stars.

Over the Lake of Flowers it is night now, it is quiet.
In the boat that carries the souls with bandaged mouths
the dead ones are removing their bandages; they untie the tight cloths
that bind their mouths. The boat is a knife cutting through the starry
    blackness.
Can you hear the water parting for its prow, its rudder
shuddering so softly where it's hidden?

That year I was sick and stayed in my room I thought of you
so tightly sealed in your glass case.
I closed the blinds and asked the sickness questions:
Why can't the light grieve?
What is the proper sowing now that there is no place for the harvest?
What is the proper sowing now that the harvest is over,
the rows moldering, the rows unkempt and tangled, overgrown and
    trampled over?
I thought of you like a dance lifted out of the dark,
whirling so fast you seemed to just stay still,
each tapering fingerbone articulate and ripe with emptiness.
And your face bandaged over, and your feet bandaged over,

while beside you the text tacked up on the wall
explained where you had gone, where you must journey,
but it was full of losses, gaps: *here the papyrus is torn,*
here it is broken off in mid-sentence.

Mummy

A jet buzzes overhead, a grating foreign music you never meant to hear
touching your bandaged skin as it passes.
An office telephone rings, an answering machine clicks on, clicks on,
while all around you the light is knifing the words "I meant never to return"
and knifing the words, "hath nursed me," and "I am far away now, journeying."
I lean above you, with my hands that will soon be nothing,
and my face that will soon be nothing, tilting in the shallow glass
        and white fluorescent lighting,
my body echoing your own as I lean further and further toward your shutness
that is saying: *here I am torn, here I am broken off in mid-sentence—*

Although It Is Daylight

Although it is daytime inside the parking garage it is dark,
the cars lined up in rows like vials
of brightly colored liquids
the grimy air has dimmed to a faint pallor.
There is no clarity here.
I listen to the clicking of my keys as I walk,
little bells, little clock-ticks
jangled and confused.

Oil drips in slick black pools beneath the cars,
not fragrant like the oils
rubbed into the bodies of the dead long ago
so they might lie in a chamber much like this
surrounded by clay jars and the small stone faces
echoing their shutness. Beside them
lotus seeds sent out three shoots
to bloom like softest cries through the hard dark
as if they could repair the stillness.
And the little statues, glazed faience or bronze,

held thumb sized baskets, sharp picks and mallets,
sacks of winter wheat for the long passage
as they watched over the dead one on its journey
so that it should not feel alone.

Now I can see the red light of the exit sign,
its bright rectangular shine. Soon the glare
of daylight will break through.
Outside, in the skyscrapers' glass facades,

each face seems distant even as it passes next to me
so closely, and I see they are not featureless at all,
though like me they're smeared gray into this daylight
where we must shimmer and move on beyond all holding
as if something very gentle briefly touched us
before it fled away.

Morning Walk

The clouds thin, dismantling their muffled kingdom.
If there is anything frantic here
it is hidden—ant-cities, leeches; there are ferns
on either side of the road, ferns tall as my knees,
and wild roses. The darkness is not powerful now,

it recedes as the light rises over the hill
and the fields open. It is a weak hemophiliac prince
too delicate to last the morning;
it will inherit nothing.
The road is dirt. I can see a car in the distance churning dust,

two heads propped up in front,
two heads anonymous as doorknobs.
It is this brown road which persists, winding the valley
and hillsides like good rope.
I learn the names of wildflowers as I walk: Stargrass, Bowman's Root,

Orange Hawkweed, Wild Indigo, Pink Aster.
I will press them in my book
so that they will look back at me one day
from a building's staticky pallors,
the fevered sizzling blur of flashing traffic. They are what remains

when the mist burns off and the storm-clouds lighten.
What I push with my fingers resists
less elliptically than sorrow: tree bark, leaves.
There is such skill in their plainness, in such direct resistance.
From the crest of the hill

it is easy to see the long fields,
the white and brown milk cows herded from one pasture
to another. What the mind fears
is itself, how it attacks itself with its cunning battalions
and clandestine maneuvers, and its spies,
its spies, its spies. Its silences

are not like this—they are hard and sharp as metal.
And the mind's sky is not blue-gold but steely white,
fiercely spiked and infinitely splintered,
or black as hysterical blindness, as if each inch of this land
had been turned over, its underneaths the only visible thing,
wormy and moist and swarming with torn roots.

Sycamore

Each day on my morning walk I see you—
gray-white among the other green-leaved trees and lilies,
stiff, cataleptic,
hardened in an attitude of writhing,
seized out of the sizzling climacteric,
witch-girl, barren sister.

With long thick trunk and bent hacked branches
you are contorted
as the escape artist found still chained
and with his heart stopped
in the locked vault
he vowed he could break free of. I am not your jailer,

though my keys jangle
in my pocket as I walk. First the fields
grew mirrory with buttercups,
then the orange hawkweed arrived
fervently lighting the green hills. Only you
remain skeletal,

marking the dirt road
with your glacial amputations, your
desperate freeze-framed dance
stripped clean of tremor. What shriek
is kept back in you, what cry? And secrets,
secrets, cold and blank as panic.

Your roots are tucked
in the moist soil and yet you starve,
your branches leafless
though the wind blows through them
invisible as headache.
The wind that makes itself visible but not in you.

What is harm
but a form of enforced stillness?
Prisoner, sister,
you no longer break and rage
but accumulate layers
of whitenesses, tight

Sycamore

mourning cloths, wrappings,
each rising wing-shadow pulsing
away from your body. How long will you stand
in this vacant, rigid trance?
What farness summons you? What grief?
In my sleep I see you burning.

From The Book of Persephone (VII)

As if the binding had broken, the binding of the beautiful book,
so I must walk through this field and that city,
down along this shoreline and over this bridge and that bridge
in order to find the lost pages . . . and can never find them all.

 Here are the burnt-orange end papers, and here the remnants of sewn threads
lifting lightly as a mermaid's tail, here the glistening doorway
of the opening sentences, and then the pages filled
to the margins with print and illustrations,
the luminous fragments lingering like a child
watching a stranger from a window
where the child's house stands alone
like the lost bead from an ancient wedding necklace,
dusty now, and chipped.

Or there are the fragments that glow with the almost imperceptible light
of the withheld: the child leaving her place at the window
to follow the stranger down an alley
because he has asked her to, and because his black coat
is like the night, and its buttons are stars
and the wind is moving through them.

She follows. As if his coat were the antidote to what?
Where are those pages that must now press like the restless
eyes of a child against doorways and window grates, stone walls,
and into the brown forks of branches,
the airy momentary stairways of blown leaves?

If the binding had stayed put, maybe it would not seem so valuable
to me now. I'd have forgotten the book, left it on the shelf,
its story a smooth and elegant circumference.
But the pages blow and blow, scattering the way terror,
long after it's been felt, still disperses and lies masked within the body.

The girl loved his coat of stars,
coat of departures, of farness, of the gold and secret
warrant of the moon.

From The Book of Persephone (VII)

There is a page for consequence. There is a page for coercion,
for fraudulence, entrapment. But the girl doesn't know this yet.
She walks with the man through the alley,
matching her footsteps to his own.
She would gather the night sky in her small hands,
the moon and stars of it, that seems so beautiful,
like a lost language that has no word for harm.

From The Book of Persephone (VIII)

The willows shed their brittle seeds.
I stand at the edge of the grove where bees sew an embroidered cloak
of buzzes, lifting it over me, dry and powdery.
There are wingbeats at my neck, quick flickerings.

In an old story a woman put on a jeweled cloak
with threads of poisoned gold sewn into it
like specks of lightning trapped and sizzling in the earth.
A gift from someone she despised,

she still found it too lovely to refuse.
But admiring herself in the mirror, she saw an eerie distance
forming on her face, the cloak feeding its hidden poisons
to her skin, then bursting into flame, a ragged claw of retribution.

When her father cradled her dead body, he, too, fell poisoned, dead,
the lightning passing from one body to another. . . .
These bees do not tire, the cloak of them rising and falling,
forming and dissolving its bright sleeves, its ebon hood

over and over, but it hides no poisons, no honey.
I am draped in a dry whirr, a fizzing music of stray embers.
White bride of distant sun!
White mistress of blank shelves, of absence!

The cloak suddenly crumbles now, unravels, the pieces
of its threads travelling, travelling. Now the foragers are flying home,
the guards waiting to let them in, their pollen baskets filled,
the fine hairs on their torsos and eyes covered with a film of pollen.

They return to their tidy compartments which nightly they clean
of old debris and fill with nectar and seal over
with fresh wax. They are disciplined as a firing squad.
They do what they must do, though their compound eyes can see the world

only in pieces, a glittery unglued mosaic.
If some don't return, the Queen doesn't miss them.
It's in her nature to hide and not grieve.
She is helpless anyway, trapped

in her closed world. When she dies or grows too old and is discarded
a new Queen will awaken, fed on royal jelly, light for a moment,
virgin, free, reeling out into the sky
where I can see her, before the mating begins, and the heavyness,

and then the long withdrawal, the retreat into the waiting hive.

The Leper Colony

Dearest Sisters, today a man in a brown suit arrived to visit us.
He wore long gloves and took our photographs to document the
    progress
of how we vanish from this earth. Also we were made to wear wet
    plaster casts
and waited calm in the bright air for them to harden their white
    hindrance
over us. When they dried he cut them from our limbs
with something that looked like a pallet knife or scalpel.
He will carry them back to the mainland to study them,

far from this promontory
thrusting its sharp volcanic rock into the sea. Far from us.
Days I watch the drawn-out wakes of steamers, their languorous
dropped veils riding the green water. Distance is theirs
and benign to them still. The passengers can't see my tiny garden
of sweet potatoes, kale, sugar beets and onions,

or how, in the black miles behind our clearing,
birds swoop and flutter from the steep, imposing cliff,
their wings cutting through this odd unanswering poverty
in which the green leaves flourish as we sicken.

Sometimes—it is hard for me to say this but it's true—
we chop our fingers off to be rid of them more quickly.
It doesn't even hurt. And after they are off us
the bloated worms still curl there, feeding.
But mostly we arrange our Sunday bonnets, and mend as best we can
our favorite frocks, the ones with bits of lace or pale cloth roses.
We garden and read and look out at the sea.

If there is self-slaughter
it is through immolation only. This only happened twice.
Who would not dream of burning?

We have started a small farm with a few cows and goats and chickens,
and last week a tiny calf was born.
I have a mongrel dog. It plays beneath the lines of drying laundry.
At night it sleeps beside me. I am not harm to it.
Its hair is coarse and dry, the color of old straw.
And trees feed on the stingless air.

What is a face but the way we travel away from ourselves,
baffled and afraid? The way we cannot stop, or turn things back.

I wake and feel my little dog beside me,
breathing, and reach to stroke its simple ears that curve like clear
    unbroken pathways
safe and cool in the deceiving air.

White Light

Seizure of light, white noise,
close-ups, zoom shots,
soundbites whizzing past the ice-white
lake of the cold floor . . . the walls jump with light
and the shadows of blocked light
lifted out of the unbodied world.

As now, on the news, a girl is running,
her hair flaming in the flickering torn flowers
of white light. Then suddenly the screen
just lets her go, the light
just lets her go, and I think of my eyes,
how strange it is to have them,
as they empty themselves so quickly of that girl
as if she were unreal.

There's black rain on the windowpane,
the glittery bits of it ticking.
I get up and stand at the glass,
my face fleshless and secretive in front of me,
holding like a placard
the silvery privilege of my watching.
How queerly flat it seems, this face,
lopped off and hanging in the icy dark,
the mouth-hole shut on nothing.

When I step back the window-square is tenantless,
though I can hear the leaves in it,
their almost-lullaby, their calm insistent pressing
into place, such softnesses as will not be turned back
bending downward in the fissured wind.

How frail my silver glance; and the body of that girl
as she ran through the torn flowers
of white light, the satellite beaming her up into my eyes,
beaming the torn flowers up and up,
the brightnesses streaming, seething from her skin. . . .
Darkness, we are brief silver coins
thrown into you

as you close austerely over us.

Airwaves

These voices cut off from flesh, from eyes,
drift now over the airwaves and over the tall indifferent buildings,
husks of cars, locust-casques of stores,
the minutes for sale, the minutes that they live in all for sale.

(I lie back and listen.
The radio's round grid of dark brown cloth
is soft where the voices touch it,
vibrating gently no matter
what horror or alarm comes streaming through it.)

The voices do not tire.
All day, all night, they empty themselves into the air,
so many of them speaking, singing; racket of laughter
and sighs, the latest news and the updates of the news.

(I watch where the window-square holds the city's lights
like stars. How frail such stalwart things can seem,
how without bearings. And the buildings,
strong and narrow as a fear of knowing,
erect a government of stone beneath the stars.)

Fright has a scarlet mind that doesn't tell
what it has seen, that doesn't know the sound of its own voice
or what syllables might find it if it speaks.
So it listens to these staticky voices
marrying the stillness over and over, it turns its face
toward a face it cannot see.

When I turn the dial to off, the lights of the digital clock
still flash the time, neon-green and heedless.
How easily the voices have gone elsewhere;
such simple tactics find them, let them go.
But fear doesn't vanish, and the body that holds it
stiffens and shudders through the hours. Fear has no voice.

Filming Jocasta

You must not show her face. Only the hands
where each granite planetary knuckle
slowly pales as if submerged in water, stripped down as after seizure,
those hands that now hold nothing.

And the rope: umbilical, predatory,
how it hangs so strictly from the ceiling
while her robes waft with such softness against the backdrop
of the palace walls, harsh walls. As if to say, But once
she was a child, once swaddled, innocent, even she,
the long ago and ever after faintly beating in each cell.

Then bring the camera closer, closer in,
it is important not to lie. And show how the robes are crevices
of riddled light, how innocence is touched
by fraudulence; there is no other story, other text.
No music to accompany her body. Only the slow turning of the rope.
Only that score that is no score, how silence is the voice
of damage, its taped mouth.

And her shadow on the wall, freakish curtain oddly beating
in the wind, blurred inscription of some lost intention;
let the camera hold it for a moment, then move on.
Here is the empty room, how large it is, how drafty.
And her smallness, for a moment, so pitiful within it;
the room like a mouth that can't speak, like the silence her body
has become, her body like a severed tongue.
And then let her body and the room become a city

where the hallowed laws are quiet, the gated storefronts quiet.
And all throughout the city's central district
there are rows of display cases, necklaces glittering
on velvet covered cardboard shaped like collarbones and necks.
Blue velvet, diamonds, gold. And rings lined up in rows,
hat pins poised like silver birds, white gloves
on plaster hands. City that turns and turns
on its invisible cold rope, and the shadows of the awful tapered hands.

No one has found her yet,
her body white as streetglare, the cold glow of the unbought
still poised there, waiting to be bought. Her hands frozen
as if molded, waiting. But still there is the question of her face,
the horrible purple, the messyness of crime.
The way the eyes bulge out like vats of half-spilled
paint, innards churning in the wind.
Not even eyes now, really, but the aftermath of eyes,
exploded. At least the frozen hands are whole,
as if some innocence remained within them even to the end.
But there was no innocence in the eyes.
And the hands cannot cover them.

From The Book of Persephone (IX)

I walk out into the buzzing field whose sky is like a book
of many pages the wind is ruffling back and forth
as it carries the smell of burning matches.
The rooftops are all far away, as if shelter were a kind of rumor.
I feel like I did as a child, when, having dreamt, and woken, and then dreamt,
I wasn't sure if I continued dreaming.

These are my eyes, and the places that have burned within them.
And here are my hands, these frantic conjectures
over the known soil. I have woken and have not woken,
as if the text were always elsewhere, the real text.

The fawn steps quietly within the dreaming body,
the trembling forest of its breath.
Is it its fear that makes it beautiful, how it must turn
its extremest attention toward each sound?
How easily startled it is, how easily the world
can hurt it. Is that why its smoothness
seems to me so much like rapture?
And then after the rapture the suddenness of shame.

Glittery windows. Footfalls and dust. I am awake and not awake.
If I keep turning the pages I will come to the one where,
I will come to the one, to the one . . . and ever after.
Long balconies softened by flowers. The mourners' black coats.
Seconds, minutes, hours. The fawn lies down within the dreaming body
and is not afraid. These are my eyes, my lips, my hair,
the dazzlement of ladders rising from the frozen ground.

These are my eyes in which the towers are still burning,
and my hands that are fortresses burned down,
flames feeding on the splintered wood.
There is the scent of jasmine swaying faintly now like lantern-glow
over the crude floors. And inside the ruined walls
so much tenderness composed or slowly savaged, so much waking
that can't quite bring itself to wake.

Lantern-light and dust. Within the dreamer, how gentle the fawn's
supple legs as it walks beside the fortress's seared walls.
Flames jump inside the fawn's dark eyes. There is the rapture
of that burning, there is the rapture of its watching eyes.

In the City of Gold Domes

Once the dream might have spoken:
torn, and without healing, or, *the blind girl sat by the lake*
consoled by the delicate stitches of water.

Things speak, then cease to speak:
white lake, frozen stars. A long sarcophagal sleep
in which the leaves slowly stiffen and unstir,
and the blind girl disappears, having left no note,
no imprint on the sand.

And then one day the dreams begin again:
When I came to the City of Lies I was entranced
by its gold domes and porticos, canals on which hibiscus flowers
floated, stone lions on the palace steps. When I saw the miners in chains

I believed they did not exist. That is what the guidebook said.
Streetlamps sifted slow gold onto cornices and walkways
and over kiosks and glass vials arranged on blankets
on the boardwalks, as sailors slipped through doorways
and cramped passageways as if they did not exist.

It was safe there, so the guidebook said.
But then why did a child vanish from its bed one night
never to be seen again, why did a blight take the plane trees,
why the women with scared eyes, the man who carried a rabbit's foot
for luck? And why the torn parasol held by a girl who couldn't speak,
the fires in alleyways, switchblades tucked into back pockets,
the Princess of the Flowers locked behind a wooden door?

The drawbridge lifts. Hibiscus flowers fade to a dull brown.
The Princess's face recedes from the window, leaving only this soft confusion
in which the city drifts and doesn't drift, while a hand dips a pen
into an inkwell to chronicle the city's history—
gold domes and hibiscus flowers harboring an azure light,
but also a child's empty bed, a torn parasol, store fires, broken doors,
and the streets where miners tread slowly in their heavy chains.

50

Walking

And now, inside the Walkman, the tape turns
in its dark compartment, carrying voices
captive and mutinous in their beauty
that will not reach the outer air.

The tape clicks and I turn it over.
A woman's voice is singing, and layered
behind it in the mix, there's another version
of her voice, sharper
and more desperate, that sounds so far away.
How it haunts the closer voice,
the way the idea of shipwreck
haunts the shining body of the newly-finished ship.

As I walk the trees harass the stillness.
It is good to see them moving, each small skirmish
of light uncautious in its barefoot passage.
And here's the rotting tree stump
where the nuthatch hunts for bugs, here the ruined fencepost
with its rusted wire, here the hawkweed orange-red in the brown grass.

In the Walkman the woman is singing of a fright
like a dry river, of how a city shone at nightfall
beautiful as any distant thing.
The poplars bend above her voice though she can't see them.
I'm bringing her into a stretch of dirt road now
where cloud-shadows shift, ghostly eyepatches, over the fields,
and noise from the expressway hovers just over the next hill.

The light can't steady itself. It quivers like her voice
fleeing a threatening stillness.
How it cleaves to each violent interruption.
How it wants to be not still—anything but that—not still.

View of the Asylum Garden

These trees feed on the stars. There is such a strong willingness in their bodies.
I look out my window and watch how the place called *outside* is made of
        many parts.
Why are the silences it leaves behind sometimes electrified, trembling
like static, and at other times serrated, cold, hard and sharp as a split geode?
And at other times spidery, skittering over the bare walls?
But always they are mirrorless, mirrorless.
I don't know how so many disparate pieces can manage to cohere

yet they cohere. The poppies, for instance, why don't they shatter
the dull surrounding grass? And the chestnut trees lifting their white veils
above the walkway, and the poplars, the stone bench—they want nothing
from each other, but stand side by side, simply, without rancor.
Together they form something larger and stronger than themselves,
and the sun comes to them, touching them harshly or softly,
each one of them the same.

If I look at the garden wrongly, fear lingers in the branches,
there are eyes and glinting needles in the leaves.
So that I think I must not be mistrustful, but let the garden guide me,
as when I was very small and I could feel the alphabet settling
bit by bit inside my body, shuddering, unfolding,
opening within me its curious inclusive arms.
How it carried me into the morning and into the dark and past the dark.

These walls are stiff as vigilance. The white curtains blow against them
and I remember not to be afraid (they are so soft),
and I remember to feel the strange comfort of all that survives.
Now someone is walking through the courtyard. I can't see his face at all,
only how the chestnut trees line the path he walks on, soft whites
and palest greens above him. I watch him pause, then stoop

to pick an iris from the dirt and slip it in his pocket.
Does he stroke it the way an infant strokes its mother's neck for comfort?
I remember seeing Giotto's frescos in Padua; how the childless man
cast out from the temple cradled a tiny lamb in his arms.
And how the other lambs gathered around him and looked at him kindly,
despite the barren rock behind him, and the rows of houses
shutting him out of their doors.

It was as if it was important to those lambs that the man still desire
to remain on this earth, and they knew if he reached out
to touch the softness of their separate bodies
he wouldn't choose to turn away from the world. . . .

Look, it is dusk now: I am so small, it is so long ago;
I can feel the alphabet sifting piece by piece into my body,
the stars of it, the grass, the abc's, the singing wind and water,
all the disparate parts falling deeper and deeper through my ribcage,
while the curtains blow and sway from the window's wooden casement,
like sentences whispering, wandering, threading themselves into the dark.

Rain

I can hear the rain now, its vanishing
averted glance, and long branches
descending softly toward cool water.
And then a voice coming back from its solitude
to find me, "When nothing spoke to me anymore
the broken statues spoke to me," and
"Be opened my mouth, untie what is upon my mouth."

I have betrayed a stillness.
I remember the statue's immaculate face,
the smooth white marble of her eyes.
And her hair so narrowly plaited
like a stringent hunger for order,
her hair like closure, the denial of regret;
how cold she was, how meticulously stranded.

Are those footsteps on the stairs now?—
a click, a jangled lock,
the rasp of cloth rubbing up against a doorway,
a rustling of sacks dropped down on a counter.
It must be my neighbor returning home from work,
and that noise—what is it now?—the drone
of a documentary he's turned on, its soundtrack

threading through the burned and looted
village, the mother and her starving child.
The music from the soundtrack touches down
onto the child's flaking skin, filters briefly, slowly down
in its momentary softness, though by now, as the film
is played, replayed, the child must be dead,
dry earth blindly over it.

The rain has stopped now, though it still rushes
in a downward motion from the trees
when the wind comes up in gusts.
My neighbor is quiet, maybe he is sleeping,
or watching how the street lamps
burn like a slow acid past his window.
I can hear the sound of the sea, though it's far off,
as if it's moved into these trees nearby us
where over and over it shatters itself to be made whole.

Thinking of the White Lamb at
San Apollinare en Classe

She stands where danger cannot find her, where danger doesn't have a face.
I can imagine no sound in her world, as if only in such silence
could she stand and not be harmed.
What's slid into me has not slid into her—she is so separate—
the rapid transit of lies, the hard glare of memory
slipping from its socket, unable to find its rightful place
or form into a clear unfractured story.
She is silent as cloth, as wind-shunned leaves. Untouched, unscathed,
far from the buzzing pinks and greens of the wrong
adjustment, the waste and throb of muted light, flickering, flickering.

But I wonder how, without mis-steps, how without faltering or stumbling,
can she know the contours of the ground she lives on.
How, without moving forward or back, without feeling the rasp of grass
against her forelegs, can she know the poppies opening below her,
or the tall white-lobed lilies stretching into sunlight
as when a face bathed in gentleness rises from the fretful
child-dark inside the body.

And yet she seems like one who has chosen to be quiet,
like a person who, after years of speaking, has simply walked
from a crowded room into an empty sealed-off garden
and is relieved not to be asked to speak.

And she is soft, soft, standing in her green detachment.
What are my hands as they move now to touch her,
what do they know, what have they done?
What history survives inside them?
What kindnesses and meannesses braided in one knotted fleshy tree?
She looks straight ahead and does not shudder, as if I must learn gentleness
by how I do not harm her,

by how these earth-bound hands go back and forth over the fine head
as a mother might stroke her child as it sleeps
there in the quiet room
where harm's delirious radiance
for a moment cannot find
the sleeping child.

From The Book of Persephone (X)

Light like nervous laughter: I remember that quickness,
and how, through a crowd, a face would find another
so briefly and in passing, as if to say, *There is a slowness
inside me even now, a place where the quickness hasn't maimed me,
and it is the pelt of a deer, a luminous brown pelt,
a deer standing in an amber clearing.*
And then the other face nods—it seems about to speak—
but the street-light flashes green and they just pass.

Now the trees settle a darkness inside them
the way a child settles words inside its body as it sleeps,
the words learned just that day, repeated over and over
until they flutter like soft birds, but hard-beaked, strong,
a clawed instinctive clinging fastening round each narrow branch.

The trees are gentle in this windless air;
I can't feel the roughness of their branches brushing up against my skin,
though when the wind starts up again, I see the treetops slowly bending
toward the river like horses stopping at a stream to drink.
The clouds come and go, come and go.

I don't know if the fawns watch this
or if they move through the forest strictly at eye-level
thinking only of not starving, of how daily the berries
grow fewer and more hard.

What is it that is not banished or lost, not abandoned?
The manes of the trees move in their soft enchantment,
above and above. I think there is a shyness in them,
something hidden they'll give only to the dark,
as when, after fits of rage, a child will suddenly quiet
and stand a long time at the window, abashed
before the serious, far stars.

Headlights

Night, and I watched from the side
of the river the cars inching forward, a line of white
headlights like the white-tipped canes
the blind put out before each step, tapping down
onto the otherness, the world. The insides
of the cars were dark, the windows dark.
I couldn't see how flesh is taken up
into the distances, enthralled by them, by the *ahead*;
only the lights lifting the silver of the cables,

the bridge's skeletal wires,
then putting them back down. How the cars bunched
at the tollbooths, one clotted edgy slowness,
while in the car at the front of each line,
a hand (I couldn't see it but of course it would be there)
rolled down the small window,
and reached out with its ticket and its bills;
the other hand opening
to receive them,

sorting out the coins for change—
the bright silver faces enshrined in each small sphere.
Quarters. Nickels. Dimes.
Then the hand rolling the window back up,
the faces floating behind it as if not attached,
as music from the tollbooth pulses over
the tolltaker's fingers drumming on the register,
and then the barrier's lifting,
letting them pass through. . . .

Now they must be moving past the landfill,
past the gulls (are they asleep? where are their nests?)
that poke down into the stinking
garbage heaps by day,
and the flames from the refineries
burning at all hours
like the flame on the assassinated President's grave.
Maybe a radio is on, yes, it must be on,
a talk show,

a voice saying Bomb them
to teach them a lesson,
      and then the click as he hangs up, the hollowness
            of air for just one second, a commercial for Pepsi,
a commercial for beef.
            Rain, guard rails, rest stops, rain, more rain,
while headlights burn through the rearview mirror
      as if pinned there, but by what?
      A hand reaches for the dial

      to keep the sound from fading,
the announcer's words breaking up in the staticky thickness
      until another voice comes on
            and then it too strays off in jagged pieces,
slurred pauses, mangled sounds. . . .
            The dashboard glows in the darkness,
the green numbers of each gauge each clock face
      glowing. The night is filled with them,
         these dashboards,

      and the eyes that turn toward the white-lined roadways
that yield so little,
      not shapes but the memory of shapes,
            as if the gods had taken back the world
and the terrible innocence of flesh
            glides forward in the sealed and heated cars,
the music playing, marking time,
      over the notion of home,
         over the riven vanished earth.

Stairways

To say "once" is to begin
a story: "Once before the wish went blank,"
"Once when I didn't ruin what I touched."

But how distant the beginnings seem to me now.
What speaks utters itself in fragments
as when, come nightfall, the stairs of the world disappear
leaving only an uneven sea of separate rooms
shimmering their tetherless lights, gold, gold,
carrying them into the hours,
the spaces between them secretive and cold.

Stairless earth, your parts drift off, edge by crumbling edge,
bearing within them their lost unspoken stories.
Where have they gone to? I can't see where they have gone.
Here are the slow drugged leaves of the night flowers,
and here the fence with its black spikes
over which the bird-cries lift and splinter, here a water glass, a table,
the radio dragging its dull tremors through the air.
I don't know what drifts beyond them.

Window-squares gleam and deepen, doors wait
at the tops of landings, severed from the floors below.
Boats sway in the river but the planks leading down
from the dock aren't there, and the stone tower
has lost its winding stair,
leaving only its smooth walls impossible to scale.

"Once before the binding broke,"
"Once when the questions glittered on the shore."

How distant the beginnings seem to me now, and the endings,
unnavigable, lost . . . .

Where are the stairways that would build themselves back into this air?
How they would slow and quell the terror, and the hallways
would wait for them, and the landings, and the doors.
How seamlessly they'd thread one place to another, one hour to another,
as when a hand reaches past its solitude, fingers opening, unfolding,

not finite and not destroyed.

Streets

The child sleeps in her crib.
Before she was born I watched through the bars of my basement windows
that cut the slabs of neon-tinctured light into small prisons,
the feet hurrying forward, and the scattered newsprint
reeling like severed wings across the pavement.

Long ago, in another city, I washed my doll's white dress
and hung it on the line to dry
where it stiffened bright and smooth with cleanliness.
The child's face in sleep is like that, so that it frightens me
sometimes—the way all wandering seems to vanish from her body.

In the chronicle of cities I hold in my hand
it says that one day not far from now
there will be just one city, and it will be continuous,
and in the end will suffer nothing but itself.
The child's child will walk there, I suppose, over the concrete
footpaths lining the long loops of highways, and through the series
of nearly-identical central squares, and the neon streets
repeating themselves endlessly.

On this page of the chronicle of cities it is written:
"Costumes, even faces, will adjust to a background of stone.
We will take the city within us into the mountains
and to the sea. We will lose the country inside ourselves
and will never regain it outside."
Even now I can feel a rigid angularity beginning to construct
itself within me, like the corner of a building,
though I still hear the rain in the trees, and the sparrows' voices
rising from a trembling background of white noise.

The child's face is a map, it is a lantern, a frail translucent page
of pencilled drawings. I gave her a name with a gentleness like rain,
a name like wind moving through an olive grove in summer.
Soon she will start speaking her first words.
In spring her father will lift her onto his shoulders and she will see
her face in the prismed glass of the tall buildings
where it will float as if lifted away from her forever
and divided over and over.

Cypresses

So much is hidden by lies. Is that why the cypresses are beautiful,
green-black and without pretense, rising plainly from the furrowed
    hillside?
They flare upward with such stark untroubled radiance,
so that it seems a strange tenderness to me
how they do not recoil, do not bend;
how they are undefeated. From far off

they are stiff obelisks, ancient funerary steles,
but up close there are small turns in them, winding crevices and byways,
briefest detours breeding in the greens.
Doorways. Pathways. Stairs. They are like eyes
that have known a harsh astonishment, yet still don't turn away
from the suddenness that claims them. Seeing them,

I think of the Chinese scholars who left their government posts
and walked off into the mountains, watching the sun rise
and the sun set, boiling some rice and water, a little gruel,
feeling the coldness seep into their bodies,
the pages thinning year by year between their fingers,
the sound of human voices growing more distant and more strange

like foreign cities in an atlas, until something like a cypress tree
rose up inside them, some stalwart spine or spire
around which the mountain-light brewed and gathered.
Or I think of the girl who can't force herself to speak,
who believes she is a lily rising from a pond's thick surface

but a brown spot is spreading on her petals,
a stain the shape of a cigarette burn or a tack, and still her petals
keep on opening, and still she can't erase the stain.
She walks to the window. The cypresses are there,
still there. And she turns her mute face to them completely
as if they knew her secret, as if they must understand

why she can't bring herself to speak
as they shine green-black and pure where she can't touch them.

The Harbor Boats

The harbor boats are taciturn. The bells echo down from the hills
in brief processions of brightness and desire, building their little songs
the way children construct ladders and cradles
from pieces of elastic string.
The bells come down from the hills like a mission of kindness,
but not to the boats, that do not hear them,

not to the buoys or the rocks. I walk the narrow inlet,
its precarious and untrustworthy calm,
though when it's still like this it seems it must always be so—
there's barely a ripple at all.

These boats don't inflict harm or suffer harm.
Old wood has whitened like salt.
Where do the harbor boats keep their neatly folded sails?
And the barnacles sticking to their hulls—hidden, barbed—
I imagine them like pieces of medieval weaponry, spiked iron balls,
unnecessary in this passive element.

On calm days such as this the air is quiet until the bells arrive.
I listen for them as for a visitor to interrupt the sameness,—
how they can alter this white sky until it's not just
blanks and blanks and blanks travelling out over the sea,
scented with sea-grass and mixing with the salty farness.

Sometimes the boats seem distant as the rigid bodies of Pompeii,
no longer desiring to unsway themselves.
They don't navigate a dizziness swirling underneath the skin.
If I were one of them, I, too, wouldn't fear the panicked
rush of crimson pulsing wildly through heart and skull.
It's calm, so calm, like a storybook nursery, this sea—

while I, who have feared my own hands, my own brain,
—each sharp unculled intention half-hidden from my overseeing eye—
walk this rocky beach where the sand roses waver in dryness
and the beach grasses bend slowly downward
like secrets released, bit by bit, into a waiting ear.

From The Book of Persephone (XI)

The furious blackout lifts and splinters.
The wind stirs the rigid stalks to bend them back and back
in wave upon wave of a most beautiful and vehement agitation;
bright yellows and brown-greens, not captive, not afraid.
Soon the white barley will poke up out of the soil.

My hands remember, my eyes remember: the long hills
that seemed a form of kindness mediating the distances,
gentle markers standing fast beneath the sky
even as sharp light beats down against them
as if possessed by a wild vindictive skepticism —
or as if it meant to break them, and still they wouldn't crumble.

I remember daylilies bright as spiking fever,
smoothest petals unsullied by travesty,
early morning undoing the blanknesses so softly,
faintest swathes of turquoise silk against a wrist,
and how the moon's slow truancy nullified the stillness.

I hear the sound of the trees, that mixture of suppression and release.
This dark has eyes. And fingers, fingers.
A forest of such plainness unfolds inside my skull, not magical, not gold.
More and more the sky unleashes its myriad underpinnings,
burglar-wind, wind of profit and loss, of recklessness, retrievals,
echoes, flight. Leaves fatten, green and supple on their bending stems.

Secrets crumble, old pillars, old regrets; they have outgrown
their strict captivity. Out of this darkness a most delicate freedom
accumulates, bright storm of rising wings that quiver and release.
More and more I watch the trees that seem so beautiful to me
because they cannot transgress what they are.

Sea

I watched the water—the stilled bay. I thought I heard it speaking,
slightest murmur and faint rush beneath the stillness, as it lay constrained
in its temporary straight-jacket, not hospital white, but a slick purple-black
as if dyed for disguise. It spoke without a mouth or tongue or voice,

like a terror-stilled face, like a burn. And then the wind picked up,
its surface shuddered and then swelled as it moved in the pantomimed
language of children—the ones who haven't yet come to mistrust their
Over and over it assembled and undid brief patterns of darkness

and light that would become discarded portraits of itself. Underneath
the fishes swam, anemones and urchins clutching and released
like fever. Fists and blades were opening, then shut. Tentacles,
locked trunks. But at sunrise the sea was a signal, the burnished surface

of a god composed of multitudes of shining bee-stung eyes. Dawn
comes and goes, like a woman rising from her bed and then returning,
the sheets softening with use and dreaming. Daylight like a pox
where the rocks lie like beggars, so publicly exposed. And at night

there's the moon's brightness siphoned off by the shore-lights
as if sickening. The low roofs of the beach houses, sleek and poised
as haunches that don't spring, that won't ever, ever spring,
while a light green fluorescence spreads beneath the landscaped

trees. . . . If we are a desperate exactitude moving like clotted traffic
over the earth, seeking a truer waywardness, an ever truer waywardness,
scouring and scouring our hands that have grown muddied, while feeling,
somehow, there is a cleanliness inside us after all, a space almost unutterably

and hurtfully clean, untouched by fraud or stubborn pettiness or mind's
infection, how can I not turn to watch you, sea, to all that is not
counterfeit in you, as you lie in your shining body no human doubt
can eradicate or alter, nor naming nor misnaming harm.

From The Book of Persephone (XII)

(SPRING)

Strange light. Its fluency drifting and glittering as fields and hillsides
display their vast economies: what is gathered from them, what is kept.
Trees dense and undeformed; daylight and night exchange places
easily as agents passing secret codes, inventions. I sleep and wake

in this, remembering a fog-thick argument always touching my skin,
even now still rife and trembling on my skin. Its song calls
as a dead child calls and calls, or, no, the way the pressure
of its absence calls: that terrible and mute instruction.

Lilies bloom satiny and pale as they lull what twists and swarms
inside me, quieting the hive. But mostly there are reds and yellows,
bright blues and greens picketing the stillness. They're sharp
in me, like fish-hooks, pins.

So little is decipherable. I watch the ragged vagabonds of leaves
blown free too early from their stems, unguarded, raw, and walk
in this wind and am one of them, set free into this fanning strangeness,
musk of heat. No parenthesis to hide inside. No cave. I am an unsteadiness

and daily become more deeply this unsteadiness, and know my face
more fully as it falters: this face that has waited in windows
as curtains blow shapelessly away from them, then correct themselves
against the wooden frames they deflate back towards and cling to.

I dream I am a birch among the plantings, a narrow scaffolding the sunlight
flickers on alchemical and hovering. White birds fly out of me and in,
erratic as rates of exchange, and their turnings are beautiful, their
openings and closings beautiful. Bright hinges. Swift calligraphy. Desire.

They fly in and out of me, their beating wings great heaves of breath,
they gather and disperse and gather, here in the migrating light that
does not sicken, and I am daughter to them, and daughter to this gathering
and this geography of voices, burnings, change.

Maeterlinck's Bees

Coming and going from the hive, they are black lines of a lie detector
printing out a graph of each evasion, each panicky deception.
How honest they are, how unconniving. Winter is long gone.
Here are the willows, the nut-trees, the violets.
The bees have flocked to them; they have built their bright metropolis,

its golden corridors and brood cells, a complex shield against derangement.
The walls shine while the princesses stir in their cribs
who for weeks lay motionless and pale,
fed in darkness, only in darkness. But now
it is swarm-time, now the palace of wax, in all its richness,

is being left by the ones who worked to fill it,
relinquishing all they've made for the unborn and newly born.
I have seen them pinned in a museum, and looked into their
compound eyes searching for some evidence
of goodness, self-sacrifice, a love of the unborn like a microscopic

blossom. But their eyes looked cold as flies' eyes, unreadable
to my human mind. What must it be like to abandon
what you've built, to willingly go hungry, leaving all your food behind?
Now the bees fly up, a jangly curtain of black and gold beads,
a shimmery exotica. What a festival this is,

this one day without labor, this complete renunciation!
For weeks they flew back and forth, predictable as a time-table,
the hands of a stop-watch wedded to precision.
But all that is over now. They are singing with relief and ardor.
They have left the honey for the brood cells, for the political

love of whichever princess will triumph and be Queen.
What fierce happiness this is, to have left behind some goodness.
Nothing is certain except that poverty awaits them.
They might die of starvation or cold, wings iced and broken
in the brittle early freeze. But nothing can persuade them to go back.

Their jeweled magic carpet is rolling and swirling through the sky.
They have nothing to hide.

Black Night

Black night severe as a frock-coat or doctrine,
there is a stiffness in you, a hardness like the moment when the radio's
switched off, and no car passes by, not a single car at all,
and the trees are stripped and ignorant of wind.

You are an injunction, a stare, a crow's wing
swerving toward a blinking, rheumy eye.
A crow's wing that will cover it, consume it.
You are the moment when fright freezes over,
fishes trapped and stunned in the black ice.

Unlike you, the days are fraught, confused, all edges and swift fissures.
I wait for them. They are dangerous but truthful.
They push you away. You with your prosecutor's sneer,
your tactics and coercions. And should I, too, confess?
And her and him and him and her? Is anyone not guilty?

Daylight busies her hands. She is scrubbing the bedposts and floors
with her candor. I wake from a dream in which willows bend and bend.
A whole grove of them, like sorrow. Nothing can make them rise.
And it was sad because the birds tried to lift them
but their bodies had turned to lead.
It's not that the willows wanted to lose their downwardness,
only to lift their branches for one moment toward the sun.

You are so cunning, always waiting in the wings, then coming out
at the necessary moment, an expert campaign manager, a fund raiser.
Bees are swarming round my wicker chair now
as if they, too, had just woken from deep sleep.
Where do you keep them, their buzzes chained like Houdini?
Look, they have escaped. Their mutinous wreathes are teeming in the sun.

February Morning

Low fog. Snow-melt. Pines. Then the things of this world brightening,
     sharpening.
I am reading William of Ockham who asked: Does one angel speak to another?
Can an angel move locally? Does the soul exist as a whole within the body?
Who asked: Can an angel move unimpeded through a vacuum and through the
     world?
On earth things are distant from each other, but in a vacuum
there are no parts, and so the angel glides easily through it, he said,
feeling no counterweight, no pull.

The sun is filling up the window now,
and I think it is like human tenderness, how it slows to hold each separate body:
the hand of a woman raw and tired from hours of scrubbing,
the crocus pushing up out of the cold untended soil,
and the doorway of the school where soon the children will be entering,
carrying their lunch bags and backpacks through the narrow hallways.

I wish I could see William of Ockham's angels
and believe in them as he did. Study them. Record them.
Their wings that can fit into the smallest of places,
their faces like the face of the butterfly
before the chrysalis begins to rip.
And how they could read each other's thoughts—of this he was quite certain.
And how they could speak secretly at times
so that only those who they chose to hear them could hear them.
And how they brought gifts to each other, not bodily,
but through thought: these are the pine trees I saw on the island,
this is the snowfall that covered the rooftops.

In 1324 he wrote in his small room, in London:
"The second problem is this: How big or how small a place can an angel
     inhabit?
The third problem is whether it is possible for more than one angel
to exist in the same place naturally.
The fourth problem is whether it is possible for an angel to pass through
the place of another while the other angel remains in that place."
In 1328, excommunicated, he took up residence in Munich
and no longer wrote of angels
though I imagine they must have still visited him in his dreams.

But what was the earth to those angels
who did not suffer its fragmentation, its precise unyielding power?
I wonder if they longed, sometimes, to be marked by it
as we are, to belong to it, to feel the white light of their bodies
slowly crumble. So that when they looked at a woman kneeling, scrubbing
a floor, or a child limping in the aftermath of the siege that claimed
his city, or a man turning a lathe hour after hour until nightfall,
they could not simply fly back up into the vacuum of heaven, unimpeded,

but would feel on their wings the human weariness, and after, the good rest,
the warmth of the small woodfire in the cottage hearth,
their too-white bodies darkening slightly with soot, the world
coming to them and coming to them, until they felt the smallest fissure
begin to form within their wholeness
to make a path where earthly love might enter.

A NOTE ABOUT THE AUTHOR

Laurie Sheck was born in the Bronx, New York, and now lives in Princeton, New Jersey with her husband and daughter. She has received many awards for her poetry, including a Guggenheim Fellowship, and fellowships from the National Endowment for the Arts, the Ingram Merrill Foundation, and the New Jersey State Council for the Arts. She has published her poems widely in such magazines as The New Yorker, The Paris Review, and Ploughshares, and has had work included in the Pushcart Prize Anthology and Best American Poetry 1991. She has taught at several colleges and universities.

A NOTE ON THE TYPE

This book was set in Monticello, a Linotype revival of the original Roman No. 1 cut by Archibald Binny and cast in 1796 by the Philadelphia type foundry Binny & Ronaldson. The face was named Monticello in honor of its use in the monumental fifty-volume *Papers of Thomas Jefferson*, published by Princeton University Press. Monticello is a transitional type design, embodying certain features of Bulmer and Baskerville, but it is a distinguished face in its own right.

Composition by Heritage Printers, Inc.,
Charlotte, North Carolina.
Printed and bound by Quebecor Printing,
Kingsport, Tennessee
Designed by Harry Ford